To:

_____

You are one of the best things to happen in 2004.

And, as you are about to discover - a whole bunch of other historic events occurred in 2004, too!

Enjoy!

Best wishes from:

_____

WELL, IT'S NO SECRET THAT THE BEST THING ABOUT A SECRET IS SECRETLY TELLING SOMEONE YOUR SECRET, THEREBY SECRETLY ADDING ANOTHER SECRET TO THEIR SECRET COLLECTION OF SECRETS, SECRETLY.

SPONGEBOB

EVENTS THAT TOOK PLACE IN

JANUARY

Top Songs across the UK and USA charts this month:

United States: "Hey Ya" by Outkast
United Kingdom: "Mad World" by Michael Andrews & Gary Jules

Events that took place in the United Kingdom

It's 2004. People are using a software called LimeWire to share music and videos (also a haven for viruses). Smartphones don't exist yet (yep, there are no Iphones or Androids). Flip phones with poor quality cameras and Uggs are all the trend. Internet is becoming more popular in everyone's homes.

Investigation of the death of Princess Diana begins.
After many delays the inquest into the death of Diana, Princess of Wales and Dodi Al-Fayed is officially opened. Diana and Dodi died in a car accident on 31st August 1997 in Paris.

The world's most prolific serial killer takes his own life.
Family doctor, Harold Shipman who is believed to have murdered dozens, if not hundreds of his patients is found hanged in his prison cell. It is believed that Harold Shipman is the UK's most prolific serial killer.

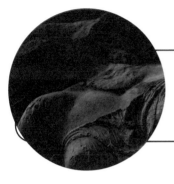

The debate over the Parthenon Marbles.
Labour politician Robin Cook expresses an opinion that the Parthenon Marbles held in the British Museum should be returned to Greece. This argument rages on for many years and it's still open until this day.

Sudden Infant Death Syndrome to not be prosecuted.
In a landmark case, the English Court of Appeal rules that parents whose babies may have died from 'Sudden Infant Death Syndrome (Cot Death)' should not necessarily be prosecuted when expert testimony fails to find any other provable reason for the death of the child.

HM Queen Elizabeth II christens the newest transatlantic liner – RMS Queen Mary 2.

The Hutton Inquiry opens investigating the death of Dr David Kelly. Dr Kelly had previously investigated claims of chemical weapons in Iraq.

 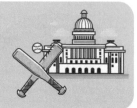

Events that took place in the United States of America

NASA's Mars Rover known as 'Spirit' lands on Mars.
Later that month its sister 'Opportunity' also landed on the planet.

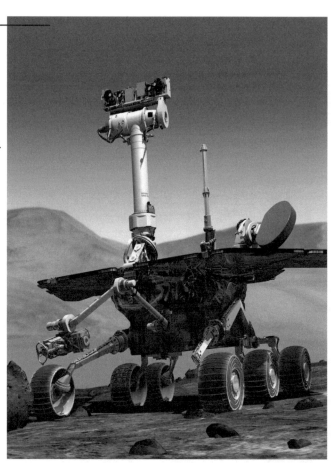

The Adventure Twins Spirit and Opportunity landed on Mars January 3 and January 24.

Both rovers lived well beyond their initially planned 90-day missions. Opportunity worked nearly 15 years on Mars, breaking a record.

The twin geologists, Spirit and Opportunity, found evidence that long ago there was water on Mars, which could have sustained microbial life.

At a hearing of the 9/11 commission, it is revealed that terrorists used mace to overpower the flight crew of American Airlines Flight 11.
To the horror of all the aircraft was later flown into the North Tower of the World Trade Centre on September 11, 2001. A day that changed the world forever.

Children's TV show Boohbah airs for the first time on PBS Kids.
PBS is also known for previously showing Tots TV and Teletubbies.

Senator John Kerry wins the Iowa Democratic Caucus.
This setback significantly impacted Howard Dean's leading position at the beginning of the selection process for the party's nominee to challenge George Bush in the current year's presidential race.

7

EVENTS THAT TOOK PLACE IN

FEBRUARY

Top Songs across the UK and USA charts this month:

United States: "Hey Ya" by Outkast
United Kingdom: "All This Time" by Michelle McManus

Events that took place in the United Kingdom

Victim Support Groups declare that the £11,000 compensation paid to the parents of the two young girls murdered in Soham by the Criminal Injuries Compensation Authority is an 'insult' and a 'pittance'.

The 10-year-old girls were murdered by Ian Huntley in Soham, Cambridgeshire in August 2002.

Critics pointed out that the £11,000 figure is the same paid as that to a crime victim who loses their sense of smell or suffers a damaged wrist.

9

Middlesborough Football Club win their first trophy in 128 years after beating Bolton Wanderers in the Football League Cup Final.

This was their first trophy since the club's formation in 1876

An enquiry is launched into the accuracy of Government intelligence centred around Iraq's 'Weapons of Mass Destruction'.

100 metre sprinter Dwain Chambers is banned from competing at the Olympics due to a positive drug test.

Events that took place in the United States of America

The New England Patriots win the Superbowl.

The half time show becomes one of the most controversial TV moments ever when Janet Jackson accidently exposed her breast during the live show.

Technology and social media giant Facebook is launched.

Facebook was founded in 2004 by Mark Zuckerberg, Eduardo Saverin, Dustin Moskovitz, and Chris Hughes, all of whom were students at Harvard University.

Starting as Facemash in 2003 at Harvard University, this online platform allowed students to rate their peers' attractiveness. Zuckerberg breached university rules to obtain necessary resources, leading to its closure after just two days.

Yet, in its brief lifespan, Facemash attracted 450 users who cast 22,000 votes, demonstrating its popularity. This early success led Zuckerberg to register the URL http://www.thefacebook.com in January 2004.

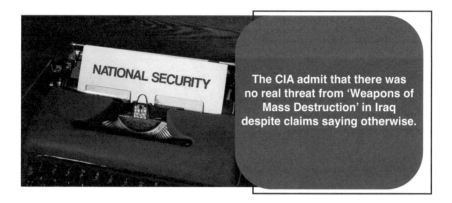

The CIA admit that there was no real threat from 'Weapons of Mass Destruction' in Iraq despite claims saying otherwise.

Peter Jackson's 'The Lord of the Rings: The Return of the King' wins 11 Oscars including Best Picture and Best Director at the 76th Academy Awards.

WHAT WAS ON TV IN
2004

On television, people are watching popular shows such as "Gilmore Girls", "Fear Factor", "The Shield", and "The O.C." in February.

EVENTS THAT TOOK PLACE IN

MARCH

Top Songs across the UK and USA charts this month:

United States: "Yeah" by Usher
United Kingdom: "Mysterious Girl" by Peter Andre

 Events that took place in the United Kingdom

● Car manufacturer, Vauxhall launches the fifth generation of its ever-popular Astra model.

Support for the Labour Party and The Conservatives is at a stalemate with neither party gaining ground.
Concerns over a 'Hung Parliament' abound as there could be an election within the next twelve months.

Actor Peter Ustinov dies aged 82 in Switzerland.
He was famous for his acting roles in Lola Montès (1955), Barefoot in Athens (1966) and Robin Hood (1973) to name a few.

15

Events that took place in the United States of America

NASA announces that Mars once had water covering its surface.

The Mars Rovers continue to send information about the planet's surface back to Earth.

Four American private military contractors are ambushed and murdered in Iraq.

John Kerry clinches the 2004 Democratic Party Presidential Nomination by winning nine out of ten primaries on 'Super Tuesday'.

1

EVENTS THAT TOOK PLACE IN

APRIL

Top Songs across the UK and USA charts this month:

United States: "Yeah" by Usher
United Kingdom: "Yeah" by Usher

Events that took place in the United Kingdom

The movie "Scooby-Doo 2" was at the top of the box office on April 1, 2004.

Pop singer Britney Spears was named FHM's sexiest woman in 2004.

Prime Minister Tony Blair announces that there will be a referendum on the EU Constitution.
This raised some questions about his future as Prime Minister.

18

The Gherkin opens in the City of London.
Designed by Sir Norman Foster, the 591ft tall building is one of London's most popular monuments - you can currently visit it through the Helix restaurant, located inside.

BORN IN
2004

Events that took place in the United States of America

Prisoner abuse is revealed at the Abu Ghraib prison in Iraq.

The final General Motors Oldsmobile rolls off the production line.

Pat Tillman, a former NFL player who enlisted for the United States army is killed in Afghanistan.

Walt Disney Pictures animated movie 'Home on the Range' is released to mixed reviews. It is the last traditionally animated picture for some years.

EVENTS THAT TOOK PLACE IN

MAY

Top Songs across the UK and USA charts this month:

United States: "Yeah" by Usher
United Kingdom: "F**k It" by Eamon

Events that took place in the United Kingdom

Internet speeds are increasing and MP3 sharing is beginning to threaten the existence of music stores.

Daily Mirror Editor, Piers Morgan is dismissed after the newspaper allegedly printed fake pictures of Iraqi prisoner abuse.
Piers lost his job due to a 'calculated and malicious hoax'. Regardless, this damaged the newspaper's reputation.

Maxine Carr is released from prison and given a new identity.
She was convicted in August 2002 for perverting the course of justice after the Soham murders.

Arsenal Football Club win the Premier League without losing a match.
Arsenal therefore amassed a total of 90 points, and had a goal difference of +47. Their points total was 11 more than Chelsea, who finished in second place with 79 points.

Children's favourite Peppa Pig airs on television for the first time.

The Simpsons premieres on Channel 4.

Events that took place in the United States of America

Massachusetts legalises same-sex marriage.

The final episode of 'Frasier' airs on NBC to critical acclaim.

"GOODNIGHT, SEATTLE"

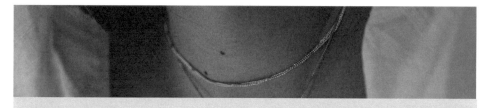

Alleged imposter and 'Saudi Princess' Antoinette Millard claims that she has had Jewellery stolen in New York City.

Sixty-six million Americans watch the final episode of 'Friends' on NBC.

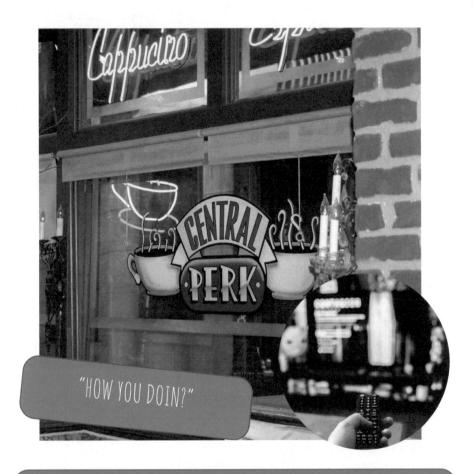

"HOW YOU DOIN?"

The show debuted 10 years and 236 episodes earlier, on September 22, 1994. Friends was a cultural phenomenon, winning six Emmy Awards

EVENTS THAT TOOK PLACE IN

JUNE

Top Songs across the UK and USA charts this month:

United States: "Burn" by Usher
United Kingdom: "F.U.R.B." by Frankee

Events that took place in the United Kingdom

Flamboyant Football Manager Jose Mourinho moves to Chelsea from FC Porto.

Mourinho made Porto FC Champions League winners, and the club in turn brought to him a new opportunity.

Meanwhile Liverpool appoints Rafael Benitez.

The 6th June was the sixtieth anniversary of D Day.

John Kerry clinches the 2004 Democratic Party Presidential Nomination by winning nine out of ten primaries on 'Super Tuesday'.

The England Football team are knocked out of Euro 2004 by Portugal on penalties.

Portugal reached the semi-finals with a 6-5 penalty shoot-out win over England.

This left England to go out of a major tournament on penalties for the fourth time.

The English team included popular footballers like Wayne Rooney, David Beckham & Frank Lampard.

 **Events that took place in the United States of America**

The first privately fund spaceplane to achieve spaceflight is flown from the Mojave Desert in California.

Ronald Reagan, the 40th President of The United States dies aged 93. A six-day state funeral follows.

In a huge step, the US led coalition hands sovereignty and control of Iraq to an interim Iraqi government.

The 9/11 Commission issues its initial findings on the events of September 11th, 2001.

WEDDING SEASON
NICOLAS CAGE & ALICE KIM'S WEDDING

Despite Alice Kim being 20 years younger than Cage, the couple were married for over a decade, and have a son together.

EVENTS THAT TOOK PLACE IN

JULY

Top Songs across the UK and USA charts this month:

United States: "Burn" by Usher
United Kingdom: "Obviously" by McFly

 Events that took place in the
United Kingdom

HM Queen Elizabeth II opens a memorial fountain in memory of Diana, Princess of Wales.
The fountain is still enjoyed by visitors in Hyde Park, London.

Gordon Brown, Chancellor of the Exchequer announces huge job losses in government departments in an effort to curb costs and to increase investment in the NHS and Education.
At the same time the government announces a review into Council Tax.

The Butler Inquiry criticises the government for its lack of intelligence when considering Weapons of Mass Destruction in Iraq.

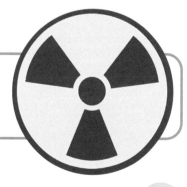

Travel Inn changes its name to Premier Travel Inn.
This pivotal rebranding, marked by the symbolic welcoming of the 'official *moon* from July 2004', signifies a new era for the beloved hotel chain, positioning it better amongst its competitors.

Marks & Spencer turn down a takeover bid by retail tycoon Philip Green.
Green sought to acquire Marks & Spencer, a move that would have majorly impacted the UK retail landscape. However, Marks & Spencer, valuing its independence and unique business approach, declined the offer.

The House of Commons' Public Administration Committee suggests significant alterations to the British Honours System.
This included scrapping Knighthoods and renaming the Order of the British Empire to the "Order of British Excellence".

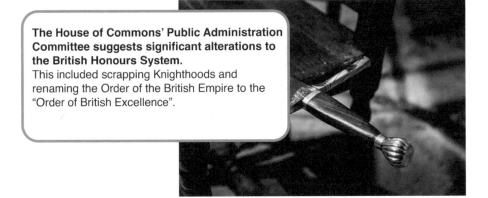

The London Crossrail project is given the go ahead by the government in a move that will improve travel links around the capital.

The main feature of the project is the construction of a new railway line that runs underground from Paddington Station to a junction near Whitechapel.

There it splits into a branch to Stratford, where it joins the Great Eastern Main Line; and a branch to Abbey Wood in southeast London.

The project was approved in 2007 and construction began in 2009. Queen Elizabeth II opened the line on 17 May 2022 during her Platinum Jubilee.

SPORTS HIGHLIGHT
WIMBLEDON

Maria Sharapova becomes first Russian player to win Wimbledon beating defending champion Serena Williams 6-1, 6-4

Roger Federer wins the second of 5 straight Wimbledon singles titles beating American Andy Roddick 4-6, 7-5, 7-6, 6-4

Events that took place in the United States of America

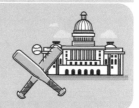

Controversial cyclist Lance Armstrong wins a sixth consecutive Tour de France.
Lance was later stripped of his titles after an investigation into doping allegations found out he used performance-enhancing drugs over his career.

John Kerry is nominated by the Democrats for the US Presidency with John Edwards as Vice President.
Future President Barack Obama delivers the keynote speech.

US indie/roots band Dispatch play a reunion concert in Boston. A record-breaking crowd of 110,000 attended.

JULY 16TH, 2004
MILLENNIUM PARK OPENING

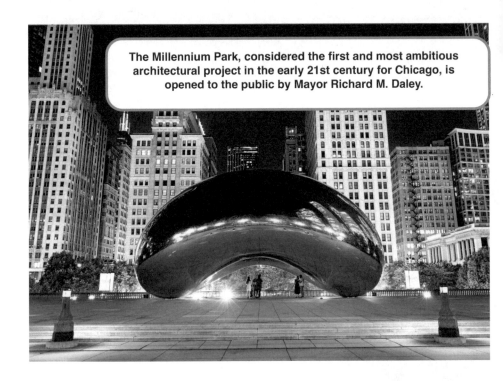

The Millennium Park, considered the first and most ambitious architectural project in the early 21st century for Chicago, is opened to the public by Mayor Richard M. Daley.

With three square blocks of open lakefront complete with a Ferris Wheel, outdoor music pavillion and ice skating rink, it becomes one of the city's most popular sites.

EVENTS THAT TOOK PLACE IN

AUGUST

Top Songs across the UK and USA charts this month:

United States: "Confessions Part II" by Usher
United Kingdom: "Dry Your Eyes" by Streets

Events that took place in the United Kingdom

In incredible scenes, Cornish village Boscastle is hit by immense flash floods causing cars and buildings to be washed out to sea.

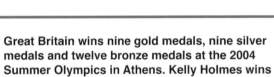

Great Britain wins nine gold medals, nine silver medals and twelve bronze medals at the 2004 Summer Olympics in Athens. Kelly Holmes wins her second gold medal.

West Bromwich Albion Football Club terminates the contract of one of its key players after he was sent to prison for causing death by dangerous driving.

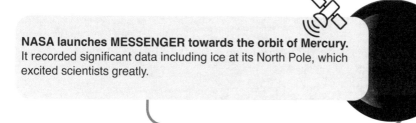

NASA launches MESSENGER towards the orbit of Mercury.
It recorded significant data including ice at its North Pole, which excited scientists greatly.

Key discoveries also included organic materials at Mercury's north pole and significant volcanic activity that was shaping its terrain. Further exploration is scheduled for December 2025.

US President George Bush and Vice President Dick Cheney are renominated for President by the Republicans.

Bush secured a silm victory over his opponent John Kerry with a margin of 35 electoral votes and after receiving 50.7% of the popular vote.

The Statue of Liberty reopens to the public after undergoing security improvements.
The statue was shut for nearly three years after the 9/11 attack.

Google's initial public offering (IPO) marked a significant event in the tech industry.

Google went public on August 19, 2004, with an IPO price of $85 per share.

It was definitely a fundraising success - Google sold 22.5 million shares and raised over $1.9 billion.

On its IPO date, Google's shares rose by 18.05%, closing at $100.34.

In 2015, an initial investment of $1,020 at the Google IPO in 2004 would have been worth more than $15,000 - a return on investment of over 1000%!

EVENTS THAT TOOK PLACE IN

SEPTEMBER

Top Songs across the UK and USA charts this month:

United States: "Lean Back" by Terror Squad
United Kingdom: "These Words" by Natasha Bedingfield

 **Events that took place in the United Kingdom**

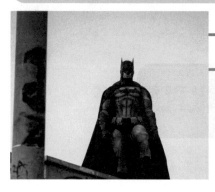

Dressed as Batman, a campaigner for 'Fathers 4 Justice', a fathers rights movement breaks into Buckingham Palace.

In a security breach, Parliament is suspended after pro-hunting campaigners break into the House of Commons.

 INTERESTING FACTS ABOUT
2004

The highest paid celebrities in 2004 were Mel Gibson, Tiger Woods, Fiona Armstrong, Tom Cruise, The Rolling Stones, J.K. Rowling, Michael Jordan, Bruce Springsteen, Steven Spielberg and Johnny Depp (According to Forbes).

Events that took place in the United States of America

'Thomas & Friends' airs for the first time on PBS Kids.
The kids TV show is based on The Railway Series books written by the Reverend W.Awdry.

The Presidential race hots up with the first live debate of the 2004 United States Presidential Election.

Nearly three thousand people are killed in Haiti when Hurricane Jeanne batters the island.

In California, a competition to produce a commercial, non-governmental renewable aircraft capable of crewed space flight known as the 'Ansari X Prize' takes off with SpaceShipOne making its maiden flight.

EVENTS THAT TOOK PLACE IN

OCTOBER

Top Songs across the UK and USA charts this month:

United States: "Goodies" by Ciara
United Kingdom: "Call On Me" by Eric Prydz

Events that took place in the United Kingdom

Prime Minister, Tony Blair confirms that he will be seeking a third term in office.

Arsenal Football Club's 49 game record winning streak is broken when they are beaten 2-0 by Manchester United.

The Selby Coalfield closes.
At its peak, the coalfield located in North Yorkshire was one of the largest ones in Europe. The closure marked the end of an era for the coal mining industry and left thousands jobless.

Princess Alice, Duchess of Gloucester dies at 102 years old – making her the oldest British Royal in history.

Atrocities continue in Iraq with further kidnapping and the murder of captives.
These acts were aimed at deterring foreign presence in Iraq and destabilizing the efforts to rebuild the country.

Afghanistan held its first democratic presidential elections.
The election of Hamid Karzai, who has been an interim leader since 2001 marked a key moment in the country's rebuilding process after decades of conflict.

 **Events that took place in the United States of America**

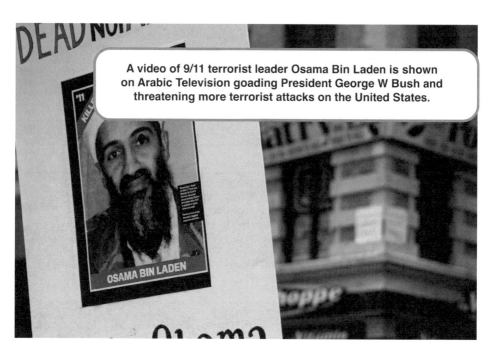

A video of 9/11 terrorist leader Osama Bin Laden is shown on Arabic Television goading President George W Bush and threatening more terrorist attacks on the United States.

OSAMA BIN LADEN

Presidential debates continue between the main candidates, George W Bush and John Kerry and their potential Vice Presidents Dick Cheney and John Edwards.

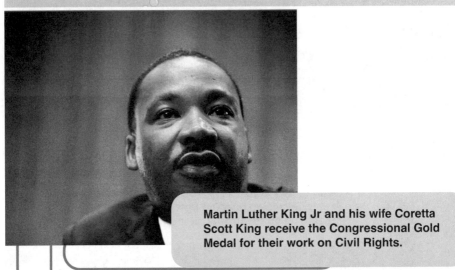

Martin Luther King Jr and his wife Coretta Scott King receive the Congressional Gold Medal for their work on Civil Rights.

Martin Luther King Jr. was a key leader in the Civil Rights Movement, advocating nonviolent protest to combat racial segregation.
Their activism directly contributed to the passage of crucial civil rights laws like the Civil Rights Act of 1964 and the Voting Rights Act of 1965.

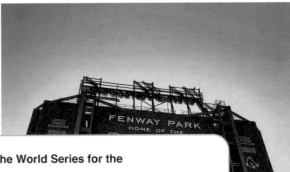

The Boston Red Sox win the World Series for the first time since 1918.
This victory was famously seen as breaking the "Curse of the Bambino," a superstition stemming from the Red Sox selling Babe Ruth to the New York Yankees in 1920.

EVENTS THAT TOOK PLACE IN

NOVEMBER

Top Songs across the UK and USA charts this month:

United States: "My Boo" by Usher & Alicia Keys
United Kingdom: "Wonderful" by Ja Rule

Events that took place in the United Kingdom

Parliament bans fox hunting in the UK causing joy and consternation in equal measures. The government also announces that smoking will be banned in public spaces within the next three years.

Sporting and music venue The Millennium Centre is opened in Cardiff.

'The Children Act' is established bringing the care of children under the jurisdiction of local directors of children's services.

The Civil Partnership Act grants same sex couples the opportunity to have a Civil partnership from 2005.

The Earl of Shaftsbury is declared missing. He was later found murdered in 2005.

At the time of his disappearance, he was in the process of divorcing his third wife, Jamila M'Barek, a nightclub hostess from Tunisia whom he had married in 2002.

The Earl's body was discovered in April 2005 in the hills near Cannes. He had been strangled to death.

BORN IN 2004

Events that took place in the United States of America

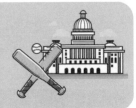

The 2004 United States Presidential election is held.
George W Bush is re-elected as President of The United States.

US Forces launch a major assault on the Iraqi town of Fallujah in an attempt to rid the area of insurgents prior to the start of Iraqi elections.

NASA hypersonic Scramjet breaks a record speed of Mach 9.6 – or about 7,000 miles an hour – this is nearly ten times faster than the speed of sound!

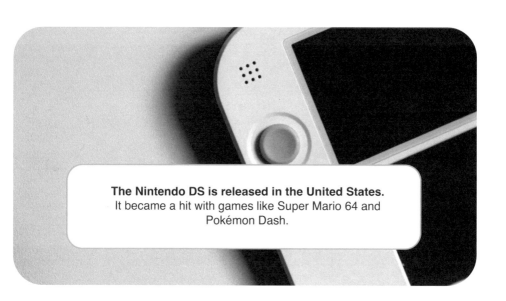

The Nintendo DS is released in the United States.
It became a hit with games like Super Mario 64 and
Pokémon Dash.

**The SpongeBob SquarePants
movie is released in theatres.**
It was one of the most popular
movies of the year.

EVENTS THAT TOOK PLACE IN

 # DECEMBER

Top Songs across the UK and USA charts this month:

United States: "My Boo" by Usher & Alicia Keys
United Kingdom: "Wonderful" by Ja Rule

Events that took place in the United Kingdom

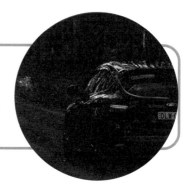

Ford launches the second version of its highly popular family car – The Ford Focus.
It's affordable price, versatile design and fuel efficiency made it a very popular choice during times of gas price increases.

A daring bank robbery in Belfast nets the perpetrators over £20 Million.

On Boxing Day, a massive Tsunami in the Indian Ocean kills thousands on surrounding islands in what is believed to be the worst natural disaster in recorded history.

Events that took place in the United States of America

Chinese Personal Computer giant, Lenovo announces its intention to buy IBM's global business in a step that would make it the third largest manufacturer of PCs in the world.

The Columbian government extradites one of world's largest drug dealers, Gilberto Rodriguez Orejuela to the United States.

Thirty-five Americans died in the Indian Ocean earthquake and subsequent Tsunami that wreaked havoc in the Indian Ocean. President George W Bush announces financial support to help the aid effort.

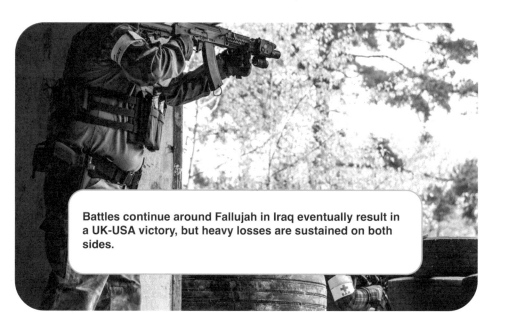

Battles continue around Fallujah in Iraq eventually result in a UK-USA victory, but heavy losses are sustained on both sides.

Fallujah was a stronghold for insurgent forces in Iraq, making it a key target for US and UK military operations. The city's capture was seen as crucial in stabilizing the region and combating insurgency.

There were two major offensives in Fallujah. The first, in April 2004, was halted due to high civilian casualties and political pressure. The second, in November 2004, known as Operation Phantom Fury, resulted in coalition forces capturing the city.

THE MUSIC EVENTS THAT SHAPED 2004

Twenty years after the original, the Band Aid single 'Do They Know It's Christmas?' was re-recorded and was the best-selling single of the year, holding the Christmas number 1 spot. The song sold over a million copies in a month.

Elton John begins The Red Piano concert residency at The Colosseum at Caesars Palace in Las Vegas. Originally scheduled for 75 performances, it will run for 248 shows over five years, including twenty-four tour dates in Europe.

The 2004 BRIT Awards are held in London. The Darkness, Dido, Busted, and Duran Duran are among the winners.

George Michael announces that Patience will be his last commercially released record. Future releases will be available from his web site in return for donations to his favourite charities.

In the classical world, Karl Jenkins continued success as a composer was rewarded by a 10-year recording deal with EMI.

The Libertines perform what would be their final concert for over 5 years in Paris, without Pete Doherty. Carl Barat then announces the split of The Libertines.

TOP MUSIC ALBUMS IN THE US

1. American Idiot - Green Day

2. The College Dropout - Kanye West

3. Funeral - Arcade Fire

4. SMiLE - Brian Wilson

5. Franz Ferdinand - Franz Ferdinand

6. Good News For People Who Love Bad News - Modest Mouse

7. Madvilliany - Madvillian

8. Hot Fuss - The Killers

9. Confessions - Usher

10. How To Dismantle An Atomic Bomb - U2

TOP MUSIC ALBUMS IN THE UK

1. Scissor Sisters by Scissor Sisters

2. Hopes and Fears by Keane

3. Greatest Hits by Robbie Williams

4.Songs About Jane by Maroon 5

5.Call Off The Search by Katie Melua

6. Anastacia by Anastacia

7. Confessions by Usher

8. Feels Like Home by Norah Jones

9. Final Straw by Snow Patrol

10. Il Divo by Il Divo

TOP GROSSING MOVIES IN THE US...

1. Shrek 2

2. Harry Potter and the Prisoner of Azkaban

3. The incredibles

4. Spider-Man 2

5. The Day After Tomorrow

6. The Lord of The Rings: The Return of the King

7. Shark Tale

8. I, Robot

9. Troy

10. Van Helsing

TOP GROSSING MOVIES IN THE UK...

1. Shrek 2

2. Bridget Jones: The Edge of Reason

3. The Lord of The Rings: The Return of the King

4. Harry Potter and the Prisoner of Azkaban

5. The incredibles

6. Spider-Man 2

7. The Day After Tomorrow

8. Shark Tale

9. Troy

10. I, Robot

SPORTING HIGHLIGHTS

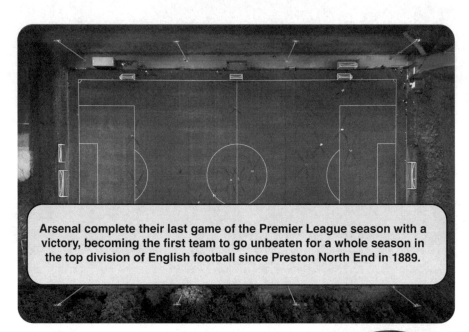

Arsenal complete their last game of the Premier League season with a victory, becoming the first team to go unbeaten for a whole season in the top division of English football since Preston North End in 1889.

91st Tour de France: no winner (Lance Armstrong disqualified).

Super Bowl XXXVIII – the New England Patriots (AFC) won 32–29 over the Carolina Panthers (NFC).

SPORTING HIGHLIGHTS

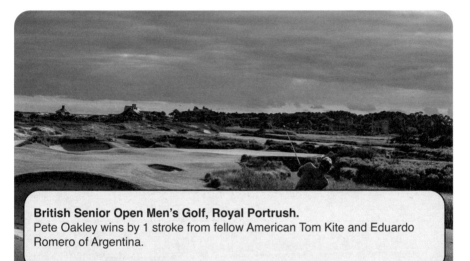

British Senior Open Men's Golf, Royal Portrush.
Pete Oakley wins by 1 stroke from fellow American Tom Kite and Eduardo Romero of Argentina.

British Open Men's Golf, Royal Troon.

American Todd Hamilton wins his only major title, defeating 2002 champion Ernie Els of South Africa by a stroke in a 4-hole playoff.

The Detroit Pistons, in a major upset, defeat the heavily favored Los Angeles Lakers, 4 games to 1. It is the Pistons first NBA title in fourteen years, and the third in franchise history.

SPORTING HIGHLIGHTS

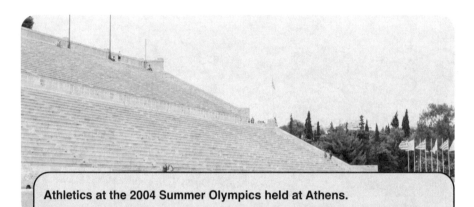

Athletics at the 2004 Summer Olympics held at Athens.

The events were held at the historic Panathenaic Stadium, which was originally built for the first modern Olympics in 1896.

The games featured record-breaking moments, such as the USA's 4x100m relay team setting a world record.

The USA snatched the most medals (total of 102)
36 GOLD, 39 SILVER & 27 BRONZE

WORLD EVENTS

Bird flu spread early this year across 10 Asian countries and regions, including China, killing tens of millions of poultry.

The NASA rovers Spirit and Opportunity landed safely on Mars, sending thousands of photos back and evidence that there once was water on the Red Planet.

Explosions hit two Iraqi mosques in March, leaving 271 dead and 500 wounded. The US television CBS released photos of US soldiers abusing Iraqi inmates in prison.

The European Union saw the largest enlargement in history when Poland, Hungary, the Czech Republic, Slovakia, Slovenia, Estonia, Latvia, Lithuania, Cyprus and Malta officially joined it on May 1.

On December 26, a strong earthquake, with a magnitude of 8.7 according to the China Seismological Bureau and 9 according to the US Geological Survey, occurred off the northern tip of Indonesia's island of Sumatra, casuing deadly tsunamis.

HOW MUCH DID THINGS COST IN 2004?

Yearly inflation rate 2.7%

Yearly inflation rate 1.39%

A gallon of gas $1.88

A gallon of unleaded £0.82

Average Annual Income $28.77k

Average Annual Income £22,011

Average Cost of a House $119,050

Average Cost of a House £146,384

Average Monthly Rent $604

Average Monthly Rent £538.50

Average Price of a New Car $21,646

Average Price of a New Car £13,000

Movie Ticket $6.21

Movie Ticket £4.49

Loaf of bread $1.05

Loaf of bread £0.65

Dozen Eggs $1.42

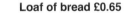

Dozen Eggs £1.56

WHAT WAS LIFE LIKE?

People were using MSN Messenger and AIM (AOL Instant Messenger) to chat with their friends online.

DVDs were starting to replace VCR tapes. You no longer had to rewind your tapes before you brought them back to the rental store - *eureca!*

The PlayStation 2 and the original Xbox were the two game consoles that competed the most with one another.

Internet started taking over the world - faster broadbands were being rolled out, allowing users to download and stream their favourite music, threatening the existence of music stores.

US President George W. Bush was named the Time Person of the Year for 2004. This was due to his election victory over Democratic Party challenger John Kerry.

YOU ARE SHARING A BIRTHDAY YEAR WITH...

MILLIE BOBBIE-BROWN

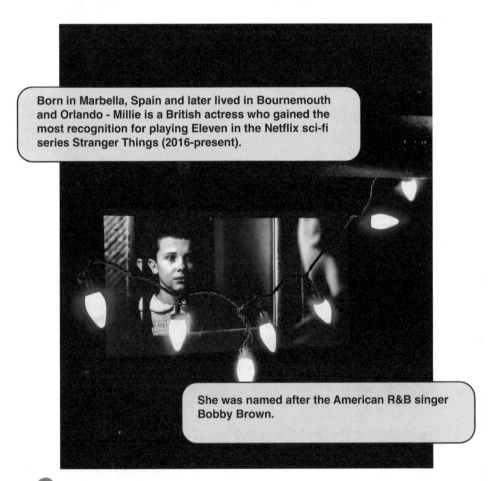

Born in Marbella, Spain and later lived in Bournemouth and Orlando - Millie is a British actress who gained the most recognition for playing Eleven in the Netflix sci-fi series Stranger Things (2016-present).

She was named after the American R&B singer Bobby Brown.

AND OF COURSE...

YOU!

HAPPY BIRTHDAY!

THANKS FOR MAKING
2004 SO SPECIAL!

THE END.

KNOW SOMEONE WHO WOULD LOVE THIS BOOK?

GET THEM A COPY!

.

Made in the USA
Columbia, SC
17 December 2024

49979474R00041